Religions Around the World

Hinduism

Anita Ganeri

raintree
a capstone company — publishers for children

Raintree is an imprint of Capstone Global Library Limited, a company incorporated in England and Wales having its registered office at 264 Banbury Road, Oxford, OX2 7DY – Registered company number: 6695582

www.raintree.co.uk
myorders@raintree.co.uk

Text © Capstone Global Library Limited 2018
The moral rights of the proprietor have been asserted.

Edited by Linda Staniford
Designed by Jenny Bergstrom
Picture research by Pam Mitsakos
Production by Steve Walker
Originated by Capstone Global Library
Printed and bound in India

ISBN 978 1 4747 4214 6 (hardback)
21 20 19 18 17
10 9 8 7 6 5 4 3 2 1

ISBN 978 1 474 74220 7 (paperback)
22 21 20 19 18
10 9 8 7 6 5 4 3 2 1

British Library Cataloguing in Publication Data
A full catalogue record for this book is available from the British Library.

Acknowledgements
We would like to thank the following for permission to reproduce photographs: Alamy: A. Amsel, 13, Choice, 15, Dinodia Photos, 17, Louise Batalla Duran, 23; Getty Images: Dan Kitwood, 26, The Washington Post, 29, uniquely india, 24; Newscom: Chris Matula/ZUMAPRESS, 5, Jack Kurtz/ZUMA Press, 14, Pictures From History, 19, Shaukat Ahmed/Pacific Press, 28; Shutterstock: Alexander Mazurkevich, 10, AlinaAme, design element, arindambanerjee, 9, AVA Bitter, cover middle, 1 middle, Calvin Chan, 22, JOAT, 16, Kertu, 11, Kristin Ruhs, 27, pcruciatti, 25, piagini raksasin, 8, PinnacleAnimates, 6 , reddees, 20, saiko3p, 12, suphanat, 21, Travel Stock, 4, Utopia _88, 18, Zzvet, 7

We would like to thank Reverend Laurence Hillel of the London Inter Faith Centre for his invaluable help in the preparation of this book.

Every effort has been made to contact copyright holders of material reproduced in this book. Any omissions will be rectified in subsequent printings if notice is given to the publisher.

Contents

Some words are shown in bold, **like this.** You can find out what they mean by looking in the glossary.

What is Hinduism?

Hinduism is a religion that began in India thousands of years ago. It is one of the oldest religions in the world. Today, around a **billion** people follow Hinduism.

The River Ganges in India is **sacred** to Hindus. Many people bathe in the water.

This famly is celebrating the Hindu New Year at a temple.

People who follow Hinduism are called Hindus. Most Hindus live in India. But many Hindus live in other places, such as Britain and North America.

What do Hindus believe?

Hindus follow their religion in many ways. Many Hindus believe in a great spirit called Brahman. Brahman cannot be seen but is everywhere. Some Hindus call Brahman "God".

The Om symbol represents the whole universe. It is a **sacred** symbol in Hinduism.

These Hindu girls in Nepal are on their way to school.

Hindus believe that it is important to worship God, work hard and look after your family. This is called dharma. Dharma means doing your best in your everyday life.

Hindus worship many gods and goddesses. Ganesha is one of the most popular gods. He has an elephant's head. He is the god of wisdom and learning. Hindus believe that he can solve their problems.

Hindus pray to Ganesha when they start something new, such as a job or a journey.

Krishna is often shown with his wife, Radha.

Another popular god is Krishna. He has blue skin to show that he is **holy.** He plays the flute and likes to play tricks on people. He is also a great leader and teacher.

9

Hindus believe that every living thing has a **soul**. After your body dies, your soul moves on to live in another body. The aim of a Hindu's life is to break free from this cycle of dying and being born again. Then, their souls can be at one with Brahman. This is called moksha.

Hindus believe that everything has a soul, including animals.

If you lead a good life, you will have a good life next time. If you lead a bad life, your next life will be bad. This is called **karma**. It means actions (good or bad) and their results.

Hindu children are encouraged to help older people and to **respect** them.

How do Hindus worship?

Many Hindus go to a **mandir** to worship. Some Hindus try to visit every day. Others only go at special times, such as festivals or family celebrations. Hindu worship is called puja.

Hindu mandirs are often highly decorated.

This is an image of the god Hanuman.

Each mandir is **dedicated** to a god, goddess or **holy** person. An **image** of the god stands in the main **shrine**. Hindus stand or bow in front of the image for puja.

When Hindus visit a **mandir,** they take off their shoes to show **respect.** Then they ring a bell to tell the god that they have arrived. The sound also clears their minds for puja.

A Hindu boy rings the temple bell.

Priests offer food and flowers from worshippers to the gods.

Worshippers stand in front of the **image**. They say prayers and give food, flowers and money to the pujari (priest). The pujari offers the food to the god to be blessed.

This shrine is **dedicated** to the god Ganesha.

Hindus also worship at home. They set aside a room or part of a room as a **shrine**. They put **images** or pictures of their favourite gods or goddesses in the shrine.

A Hindu family worships at a shrine in their home.

In Hinduism, there are no set times or days for puja. Many Hindus choose to worship in the early morning when it is peaceful and quiet.

Sacred texts

There are many **sacred** texts in Hinduism. The oldest are called the Vedas. They include many prayers and poems that praise the gods. They also teach about Hindu beliefs.

In a mandir, a priest reads from the sacred texts.

The sacred texts are written in Sanskrit, an **ancient** Indian language.

At first, the prayers and poems were not written down. People learned them by heart, then passed them on to others. Later, they were written down in an ancient language called Sanskrit.

19

Another **sacred** text is the Mahabharata. It is a very long poem. It tells the story of a battle between two royal families. Krishna teaches one of the royal princes about doing his best.

This scene from the Mahabharata shows a chariot fight.

The Ramayana story is often performed as a dance.

The Ramayana is a poem that tells the story of the god Rama and his wife, Sita. Sita is kidnapped by an evil demon called Ravana. Rama kills Ravana and rescues Sita.

Special times

There are many special times in a Hindu's life. When a baby is about a year old, he or she has a first haircut. Hindus believe that this takes away any bad **karma** from a past life.

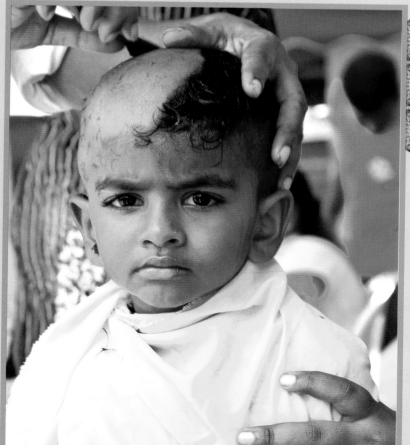

The hair that is cut off is sometimes offered to the gods.

The sacred thread on the boy's wrist represents his promises to **respect** his parents and community.

When a boy is ten years old, a **ceremony** is held in the **mandir**. It marks the end of his childhood and the start of his adult life. He is given a long loop of **sacred** thread to wear.

At a Hindu wedding the couple make seven promises as they walk around a sacred fire.

A Hindu wedding takes place around a **sacred** fire. During the **ceremony**, the couple take seven steps around the fire. With each step, they make a promise to each other.

When a Hindu dies, his or her body is **cremated** on a huge fire made from wood. Later, the ashes are scattered in a river. Hindus believe the water washes away people's bad **karma**.

After a funeral, there are 10 to 12 days of **mourning**.

Hindu festivals

There are hundreds of Hindu festivals in the year. Divali, the festival of lights, falls in October or November. At this time, many Hindus remember the story of Rama and Sita that is told in the Ramayana.

At Divali, Hindus light little clay lamps called divas to guide Rama and Sita home.

At Holi, as well as throwing coloured paint, people dance and sing.

Holi is celebrated in March or April. People throw paint and coloured water at each other, to remember the god Krishna's tricks. They light bonfires and burn **models** of Holika, a wicked witch.

A brother and sister make promises to each other at Raksha Bandhan.

Raksha Bandhan in August is a happy time for brothers and sisters. A sister ties a brightly coloured bracelet around her brother's wrist. In return, he promises to look after her.

Janmashtami is another August festival. This is when Hindus celebrate Krishna's birthday. They place an **image** of baby Krishna in a cradle and take turns to rock the cradle.

Janmashtami celebrations last for two days. During this time Hindus act out scenes from Krishna's life.

Glossary

ancient from a long time ago

billion one thousand million; one followed by nine noughts

ceremony special actions, words or music performed to mark an important event

cremate burn a dead body to ashes

dedicate devote to the worship of a particular god, goddess or holy person

holy sacred, dedicated to a god or goddess

image representation of someone or something

karma actions, good or bad, and the result of these actions, good or bad

mandir Hindu temple

model something that is made to look like a person or object

mourning being very sad and missing someone who has died

respect feeling of admiration or high regard for someone or something

sacred holy, deserving great respect

shrine place that contains objects associated with a holy person

soul part of a person you cannot see, sometimes called the spirit

Find out more

Books

Celebrating Hindu Festivals (Celebration Days), Liz Miles (Raintree, 2015)

Holi (Festivals Around the World), Grace Jones (Booklife, 2015)

We are Hindus (My Religion and Me), Philip Blake (Franklin Watts, 2015)

Websites

www.bbc.co.uk/schools/religion/hinduism/
Find out more about Hinduism with this fact-packed website.

www.primaryhomeworkhelp.co.uk/religion/hinduism.htm
Lots of information about Hinduism to help you with homework projects.

Index